BOCUSE
A LA CARTE

BOCUSE
A LA CARTE

by Paul Bocuse

translated from the French by Colette Rossant

PANTHEON BOOKS, NEW YORK

Introduction

My profession makes me think of a play on which the curtain rises twice a day. I have also compared my restaurant to a boat that must sail at noon and again in the evening. Its passengers are my guests and should feel at ease. As long as I am their host, I am responsible for their well-being. If you simply cook for your family and friends, this timing and these obligations are yours as well, and you don't need a long menu like the one from my restaurant to make people happy. Nor is it necessary to prepare costly and complicated dishes for a successful meal. You don't even need to master a large number of recipes to become known as a good cook. You all have friends at whose homes you dine with the greatest pleasure because they prepare a particularly delicious *boeuf bourguignon* or an extraordinary *blanquette de veau*.

This is why I am giving you a choice of thirteen menus to prepare at home: easy recipes with short, clear directions that anyone can follow. This is real food, simple food, a traditional cuisine that, with several more elegant recipes for holiday and party meals, has been chosen from among the most famous recipes of my restaurant. If you know how to prepare these meals, you'll be ready for any occasion, especially since the recipes are accompanied by advice on marketing, wines, and ingredients; little stratagems that help simplify preparation; and ideas for modifying recipes by using produce and ingredients readily available at the market.

The market: that's the key word. If I called my first book *La Cuisine*

du Marché* (Cuisine from the Market), it is because I believe that the quality of the ingredients is the foremost consideration in cooking well. Preferably, each cook should use regional ingredients, those that have traveled the shortest distance to reach the market. This word of advice will allow you to produce successfully a great number of dishes that depart from the recipes given here. You will discover for yourself that a certain soup or fish, made with different vegetables or fish according to the season and availability, will become an entirely new dish. You should also know how to shop, to recognize the quality of a cut of meat or the freshness of a fish just by looking at it, know which fruit is tastiest in which season.

In Lyon, no meal is complete without wine. It doesn't have to be a great wine; simple country wines that complement home cooking often offer you the best value for your money.

When your shopping is done and you're in the kitchen to begin preparing the meal, you may wonder what utensils to use. If you own a

*EDITOR'S NOTE: Published in the United States as *Paul Bocuse's French Cooking*.

food processor, you may find it useful, but you don't need the last word in kitchen gadgets to create a fine meal. For example, I always cut vegetables with a knife. They end up being just as tasty, even if they aren't cut as finely as with an electric appliance.

The dish is cooked and ready to serve. In these pages, you will not find prearranged, individual servings for each guest. Service on plates, as we professionals call it, is not appropriate for a meal enjoyed at home. What could be more delightful than a large platter upon which the meat is arranged, surrounded by vegetables, or more tempting than a bowl full of thick cream from which each guest may serve himself according to his appetite or desire! So don't hesitate to take a dish directly from the oven and lift off the lid before your guests. It smells so good . . . now you can enjoy your heartwarming meal. *Bon appétit!*

First American Edition

English translation Copyright © 1987 by Random House, Inc.

All rights reserved under International and Pan-American Copyright Conventions. Published in the United States by Pantheon Books, a division of Random House, Inc. New York, and simultaneously in Canada by Random House of Canada Limited, Toronto. Originally published in France by Flammarion et Cie, Paris, in 1986. Copyright © 1986 by Flammarion.

Printed in France

Library of Congress Cataloging-in-Publication Data

Bocuse, Paul, 1926–
 Bocuse à la carte.
 Translation of: Bocuse à la carte.
 1. Cookery, French.   2. Menus.
 I. Title
TX719.B6715 1987 641.5 87-43021
ISBN 0-394-56267-4

Contents

My Day in Lyon

My restaurant is located in Collonges-au-Mont-d'Or, on the rue de la Plage, a few miles from the center of Lyon, where my great-grandfather used to serve the fishermen and bathers of the nearby Saone River. Times have changed, yet I cling to my forefathers' habits: I rise early each morning to do my shopping at the vegetable market, on the quai Saint-Antoine in central Lyon. I enjoy my first cup of espresso in a little bistro which is always lively at that early hour, then off I go to choose fish, meats, cheeses, butter, and cream at the marketplace called Halles de la Part-Dieu.

A second coffee break, after which I walk through the garden where we grow vegetables, flowers, and herbs for our kitchen. Later, I visit the abbey, where marriages, banquets, receptions, and various celebrations take place to the accompaniment of an organ, and where ice cream and sherbets are served from an all-weather cart.

A wine-tasting session with the *sommelier* follows a few autographs given to guests. Finally, the family lunch. The day has not ended—business and administrative affairs take up much of my time and, of course, I am often tied up on the telephone.

Shopping

Here are some rules of thumb to guide you in your shopping. They are important because your cooking should be geared to the market. In planning your menu, let yourself be guided by the market's offerings and the season's produce; you will be surprised at the higher quality of your dishes.

Meat

The success of any meat recipe depends on the choice of cut. There are

Veal is quite pale, almost white to light pink for the highest grades, deeper pink for the lesser grades.

Beef is bright red (or ruby-colored) for the highest grades, darker for other grades, depending on how long it has been aged.

Lamb of good quality is pale pink; mutton varies from bright red to dark red.

Pork should be lean with a bright pink hue.

hen when she has stopped laying eggs (she weighs about 4 to 6 pounds) and is called a **roaster** when she has just begun to lay

two categories of meat: those that can be roasted and broiled and those that should be boiled or braised. You should buy whichever cut of meat is appropriate to the chosen recipe; you cannot broil a cut intended for slow braising.

Poultry
I tend to use Bresse chickens* or free-range poultry in my cooking, rather than ordinary mass-produced chickens. If you must buy the latter, choose a young one (but not too small), with a smooth white skin. A female chicken is called a

*EDITOR'S NOTE: These chickens, raised near the city of Bresse in Normandy, are famous for their excellence.

(weighing between 3½ and 5½ pounds). A **capon** is a castrated male chicken that is fattened before slaughter. When choosing a turkey, look for a plump bird with white fat and dark-colored feet; a duck, too, should be plump with white fat and dark-colored feet, but not too young or it will be bland (I prefer Barbary ducks). A guinea hen should have very pale flesh. Don't forget rabbit, a good substitute for many poultry recipes; it should be plump, quite fatty, and white-fleshed.

Variety meats
Variety meats play a very important part in French cuisine. Make sure that they are as fresh as pos-

sible and cook them without delay, since they spoil easily.

Game
Hare, pheasant, partridge, woodcock—for my taste, game need not be hung. You can perfectly well enjoy freshly killed partridge. But if you prefer game that is hung, place unplucked or unskinned game in a cold cellar or in the refrigerator. You can keep the game for five to six days, skinning or plucking the animal just before preparing and cooking it.*

*EDITOR'S NOTE: In the United States, pheasants are raised on farms. Partridges are often frozen; defrost overnight in refrigerator.

Vegetables and herbs

Ideally, vegetables should go right from the garden to the table. They should be cooked until firm but tender to the bite in a large quantity of salted water, then rinsed under cold running water and drained. Aromatic herbs enjoy more and more popularity as we find them fresh all year long in many markets, but you can easily grow the most essential herbs on your windowsill.

Fish and seafood

As I was born near the Saone River, I am particularly fond of freshwater fish: pike, perch, trout, eel, and tiny fish for frying. However, ocean fishing brings excellent saltwater fish to the market as well: sole, turbot, cod (which can be dried), anglerfish, mackerel, herring, sardines, whiting, mullet, tuna, red mullet, and sea perch. Finally, don't forget shellfish: lobster, rock lobster, crab, spider crab, crayfish, shrimp, and others. For all, a single rule applies: as fresh as possible. Find and put your trust in a reputable fishmonger.

Leek and potato soup

To begin, here is a savory leek and potato soup, one of my favorites. Nowadays, we appreciate simple, rustic food. It is honest cooking and the taste of fresh ingredients should dominate.

My leek and potato soup is a perfect example. Its principal ingredient is the leek, a relatively inexpensive vegetable available year-round. Winter or summer, it is always good for you. With this recipe, you can create other soups simply by adding squash, turnips, cabbage, cauliflower, or peas.

Bass in pastry

This recipe is one of the great success stories of my restaurant, and the way I've prepared bass for more than thirty-five years. As the fish is stuffed with lobster mousse it is a bit expensive, but it is a perfect dish to please guests at a dinner party. If you don't want to spend so much, you can use fresh herbs for the stuffing. Tarragon, dill, parsley, or chervil, to name only a few, lend an exquisite flavor to this dish. You can also use a large red snapper or salmon in place of the bass.

Be sure to leave your dough in the refrigerator until you are ready to use it. It is impossible to work with it at room temperature.

Oranges with orange sauce

This is a marvelous dessert that is easy to prepare. Its flavor comes not only from the oranges themselves but also from grenadine syrup. Grenadine is the deep red juice of the pomegranate. This bittersweet juice is boiled with sugar to form a syrup that is often used for mixed drinks. It is added to this recipe not only for its taste but for the lovely red hue it gives to the fruit. The navel orange (a large, thick-skinned orange) seems to me best suited for this recipe. It reaches its peak of flavor during the months of December, January, and February. I also like to use fresh pistachios imported from Sicily.

LEEK AND POTATO SOUP
Soupe poireaux–pommes de terre

Ingredients for 4 people:

3–4 medium-sized leeks
3 tablespoons unsalted butter
sea salt
1 pound potatoes
1½ quarts cold water
6 tablespoons *crème fraîche* or heavy cream
1 bunch fresh chervil
freshly ground pepper

Method:

1. Wash and thinly slice the leeks.
2. Melt butter in a saucepan and sauté the leeks. Season with salt.
3. Add the potatoes, peeled and sliced.
4. Add the water and boil over high heat for 15 minutes.
5. Lower the heat and add the *crème fraîche* and sprigs of chervil. Season with pepper to taste.
6. Adjust seasoning and serve immediately, perhaps with a few croutons and grated Swiss cheese.

BASS IN PASTRY
Loup en croûte

Ingredients for 4 people:

1 sea bass (about 3 pounds), cleaned and
  ready to cook
sea salt
freshly ground pepper
1 tablespoon olive oil

FOR THE STUFFING:

7 ounces raw lobster meat
sea salt
freshly ground pepper
pinch of nutmeg
¾ cup *crème fraîche* or heavy cream
¼ cup chopped pistachio nuts
1 small can truffles (optional)
1 pound puff or flaky pastry (1 package
  frozen puff or flaky pastry, thawed)
1–2 egg yolks

Method:

1. Carefully remove the skin of the
bass and sprinkle the fish with salt
and pepper, drizzle with olive oil.

2. Puree the lobster flesh (it should
be very cold) and add salt, pepper,
and nutmeg to taste. Place in a chilled bowl.

3. Beat in the heavy cream and add
the pistachios and truffles cut into
very small pieces.

4. Stuff the bass with the lobster
mixture.

5. Divide the pastry dough in
two, roll out each sheet, place the
bass on top of one, cover the fish with
the other, and seal the edges by
pressing with your fingertips.

6. Cut off the excess dough, leaving
enough to simulate the fins. Use a
spoon to mark out scales, and with
the remaining dough, simulate the
gills and the eye.

7. Place the fish on a cookie sheet
and brush the dough with beaten
egg yolk.

8. Bake the fish in a preheated 425°
oven for 10 minutes, then reduce
the heat to 350° and cook for 25 to 30
minutes longer. Remove from the
oven and serve immediately.

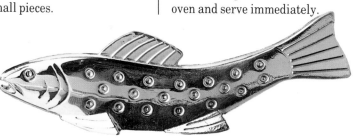

ORANGES WITH ORANGE SAUCE
Oranges à l'orange

Ingredients for 4 people:

4 large oranges
⅓ cup grenadine syrup
2 tablespoons brown sugar
pistachio nuts

Method:

1. Wash, then peel the oranges with a vegetable peeler. Cut the largest zests into very fine julienne.

2. Place the julienned zest in a saucepan containing the syrup. Add the sugar.

3. Boil the zest over medium heat.
4. Meanwhile, remove the white pith from the oranges, cut out sections without membrane, and sprinkle the orange sections with juice squeezed from the remaining flesh.
5. Arrange the orange sections in a serving dish, pour over the syrup with the zests, sprinkle with pistachios, and serve.

You may know how to clean leeks, but perhaps my method will make the task easier for you.

To begin with, slice off the very end of the bulb where the roots grow. Then, with a small sharp knife, cut away a part of the green leaves; not too much, for the leaves give the soup a lovely green color. Now, halve the leeks lengthwise from the bulb back to the leaves. In principle, this vegetable should be washed in very hot water so that the embedded

releases their juices to flavor the soup. If you do not have excellent tap water in your area, use nonsparkling mineral or spring water.

A few rules should be observed when choosing the fish. A fresh fish has clear eyes, red gills, firm flesh, and moist fins. This recipe calls for

removing the skin of the bass; not an easy task, but one that can be achieved by an amateur, provided that the fish has not been scaled. The skin of an unscaled fish is easier to remove.

First, split the skin along the dorsal spine. Cut carefully around the gills. When half the skin is loose, pull hard toward the tail to remove the rest. Repeat the procedure for the other side. If this seems too difficult, ask your fishmonger to do it for you. A kind word will surely persuade him.

Whoever tastes this delicious dessert will include it often in his or her meals. The successful marriage of the sweet and sour taste of grenadine and the slightly spicy, bitter flavor of the zest will earn you compliments. Be careful not to use the white pith, which can be bitter. You should cut all of it away. First, slice off the very top and bottom of the orange, then, holding the orange vertically, cut away deeply the peel and white pith from top to bottom. Only the fruit's flesh will remain. You can now cut out sections between the natural membrane separations. Don't forget to squeeze the remaining flesh adhering to the peel. A drop of orange liqueur added right before serving will enhance the taste.

arth is rinsed off more easily and the leeks can then be cut. Sprinkle them with salt and sauté them in butter without browning them; this

15

Marinated mushrooms

This recipe is fast and easy. The mushrooms should be fresh, firm, and white, with tightly closed caps.

The mushrooms are washed, then marinated. The short cooking time preserves their flavor. You can serve the mushrooms slightly warm or chilled. This dish can be prepared ahead of time or even the day before, which is a plus when you have little spare time.

A tip: use extra-virgin olive oil for the fullest flavor; it is truly the best.

Sautéed lamb

My sautéed lamb will win over even the most resolute lamb haters. It is vital to choose young lamb, not mutton. You can recognize lamb by its pale red color and its very white fat. Mutton is darker red with fatty gristle and a rather strong flavor that some like and others do not.

The best European lamb comes from animals that have grazed on the salty prairies near the English Channel. Lamb from the Alps is also highly regarded.* You should find a reputable butcher in whom you have total confidence.

For this dish, you'll need a boned shoulder of lamb. Don't worry if you can't find some of the vegetables. You can even prepare this dish with potatoes alone; it is always delicious.

*EDITOR'S NOTE: In the United States, the best lamb available comes from Australia and New Zealand.

Caramel custard

This dessert requires a rather lengthy preparation, but it will be well worth your efforts. Make the custard the night before for easy unmolding. To unmold, place a serving dish over the custard and turn it upside down in one abrupt movement.

The custard owes its creaminess to its lengthy baking in the oven; it should be smooth throughout and will attain this consistency only if baked very slowly. The caramel should be light in color or else it will be bitter.

I have chosen vanilla as a flavoring, but you may use rum or another flavoring to vary the recipe. Use your imagination and try whatever your fancy dictates. One more word of advice: break the eggs one by one on the edge of the counter or of a bowl and add them all at once. Be sure that no eggshell bits cling to the eggs before you drop them into the bowl.

MARINATED MUSHROOMS
Champignons à la grecque

Ingredients for 4 people:

1 pound small white mushrooms
sea salt
freshly ground pepper
juice of 1 lemon
1 cup white wine
pinch of thyme
1 small bay leaf
10 coriander seeds
1 large tomato, peeled, seeded, and
   coarsely chopped
⅓ cup chopped parsley
⅓ cup olive oil
1 large onion, coarsely
   chopped

Method:

1. In a large bowl, place washed mushrooms, salt, pepper, and lemon juice.
2. Add the white wine, thyme, bay leaf, coriander, tomato, and parsley. Combine and set aside.
3. In a skillet heat the oil until very hot, sauté the onions until transparent but do not brown.
4. Add the mushroom mixture, bring to a rapid boil, and cook for 5 minutes.

5. Pour immediately into a bowl to interrupt cooking. Serve warm, or refrigerate and serve chilled the following day.

SAUTÉED LAMB
Sauté d'agneau

Ingredients for 4 people:

½ pound lamb neck, boned
1¾ pounds lamb shoulder, boned
sea salt
freshly ground pepper
1 pound potatoes
½ pound pearl onions
1 bunch spring onions
1 small bunch baby carrots or
    about 4 young carrots
3 turnips
2–3 celery stalks
4 small tomatoes
3 tablespoons olive oil
1½ ounces cognac
2 cups white wine
2 cups cold water
4 garlic cloves
½ bay leaf
a few sprigs thyme
¼ pound peas
¼ pound string beans

Method:

1. Cut the neck and shoulder into large chunks.
2. Sprinkle the meat with salt and pepper, rub in well and allow to penetrate.
3. Meanwhile, peel the potatoes, clean the spring onions, and cut both into chunks.
4. Peel the pearl onions, carrots, and turnips; wash the celery and tomatoes.
5. In a large, heavy saucepan, heat the oil and brown the meat. Add the vegetables.
6. Moisten with the cognac, then add the wine and water.

7. Add the garlic cloves, unpeeled, the bay leaf, and the thyme; cover the saucepan and simmer for about an hour.
8. Add the peas and beans and allow to simmer, covered, for 15 to 20 minutes more.
9. Arrange in a large serving bowl, sprinkle with pepper, and serve.

CARAMEL CUSTARD
Crème caramel

Ingredients for 4 people:

8 egg yolks
4 whole eggs
¾ cup sugar
2 vanilla beans
1 quart milk
4 sugar lumps
2–3 tablespoons cold water

Method:

1. Beat together the yolks, the whole eggs, and the ¾ cup sugar.
2. Split the vanilla beans and scrape the insides with a knife. Add the scrapings to the milk, then beat the milk into the egg mixture.

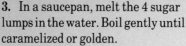

3. In a saucepan, melt the 4 sugar lumps in the water. Boil gently until caramelized or golden.
4. Immediately pour the caramel into a large ovenproof ramekin and pour the egg-milk mixture over it.

5. Cover the bottom of a large ovenproof saucepan with a sheet of wax paper, place the ramekin inside the saucepan, and fill the saucepan with water ¾ up the sides of the ramekin. Bring the water to a boil.

6. Slide the *bain-marie* into a preheated 300° oven and bake for 1 hour and 20 minutes to 1½ hours.
7. Remove the ramekin, allow to cool, and refrigerate overnight.
8. When ready to serve, unmold the *crème* onto a plate.

or this sautéed lamb, I use a
pecial saucepan with a concave lid,
vhich I fill with cold water or ice
ubes. While the meat cooks, the
team inside the saucepan liquifies

n contact with the cold lid and the
rops fall back onto the meat. If you
on't own this type of pan, you can
reate one by covering your sauce-
an with a heatproof plate. This
nethod is well worth the effort,
ince the meat cooks in its own
uices and the result is always
elicious.

Turnip Roses

You may not have used all the turnips in the bunch you bought to
make the sautéed lamb. Transform
those that remain into roses or teach
your children how to do it; it will
amuse them and introduce them to
cooking. It's never too late to in-

terest them in the preparation of
their favorite dishes.

First, remove the leaves, if any,

from the top of the turnip and peel
it. The outer petals of the roses are
whittled around the edge of the veg-

etable with a small sharp knife. Cut
away some of the flesh at each curve.

Continue in concentric circles toward the center of the turnip until
all the rose petals are formed. Tint
the turnips red with food dye or red
wine, but leave one white rose for
contrast.

Bain-marie

A *bain-marie* is a large pan or other
receptacle filled with boiling water
into which is placed a smaller dish
containing the food to be heated or
lightly cooked. It is similar to a dou-
ble boiler since the mixture being
prepared can be heated slowly without being brought to a boil or burned.

You have surely been annoyed to
find that the water in your *bain-
marie* has spilled over the sides and
spoiled your custard. I have a trick
for avoiding this: cut a circle from a
sheet of paper (preferably wax

paper, but even newspaper will do)
and place it at the bottom of the pan
before adding the water. Bring to a
boil before inserting the smaller
dish and placing in the oven.

21

Onion soup

This soup is a great classic of the cuisine of Lyon. We usually serve it *au gratin*. The garnish of toasted rounds of bread and grated Swiss cheese assures its perfection.

For this recipe, you must slice the onions thinly. In the winter, I use golden onions; as soon as spring arrives, I use white onions or new spring onions, which give the soup a different flavor. However, I never use the large Spanish onions, which I find too sweet. Sauté the onions until golden, but do not let them brown or they will be bitter.

For an even mellower taste, you can add an egg yolk beaten with a little port wine to the soup just before serving. You may also pour the soup into an ovenproof soup tureen, add toast rounds and grated Swiss cheese, and broil in a very hot oven.

Stuffed veal roast

This is a veal roast stuffed with kidneys. It makes a wonderful Sunday dinner to share with family or friends.

The quality of the ingredients, especially of the kidneys, is important to the success of the dish. The kidney should be fresh and still covered with its pure white layer of fat. Kidneys are recognizably fresh when they are a light color; if they are dark red, don't use them.

The veal you buy should be a clear, pale pink. If any fat shows, it should be white and, like the meat, very firm.

I find that a dry white wine, such as a Saint-Véran, adds just the right flavor to the roast.

Chocolate mousse

Here is a favorite dessert among children and one that can be made well ahead of time, as it only improves in flavor.

You can freeze as well as refrigerate the mousse. Frozen, it resembles a smooth, very light ice cream.

It is advisable to use dark or bittersweet chocolate; the best mousse is made with cocoa from Latin America. There are even vintage cocoas, just as there are vintage wines. You can find bars of excellent dark chocolate in fine gourmet and specialty food stores.

It is easier than you think to prepare this chocolate mousse. You simply follow the directions carefully and measure the ingredients precisely. Serve the mousse sprinkled with grated chocolate and just a dab of whipped cream.

ONION SOUP
Soupe à l'oignon

Ingredients for 4 people:

3 large onions
3 tablespoons butter
sea salt
1–2 tablespoons flour
1½ ounces cognac
2 cups white wine
5 cups water or bouillon
freshly ground pepper
slices of French or Italian bread, toasted
½ cup grated gruyère or Swiss cheese

Method:

1. Peel and thinly slice the onions.
2. Melt the butter in a large saucepan and sauté the onions until transparent but not brown.
3. Add salt to taste, sprinkle with flour, moisten with the cognac and white wine, and add the water or bouillon.
4. Boil 20 minutes, pour into individual bowls, and season with pepper.
5. Arrange the toasted bread on top of each serving and sprinkle with cheese. If desired, broil until golden brown.

STUFFED VEAL ROAST
Rognonnade de veau

Ingredients for 6 people:

1 bunch spring onions
4 carrots
4 tomatoes
4 garlic cloves
1 *bouquet garni*
5 pounds veal rib roast (or shoulder), boned
1 whole veal kidney, fat intact
sea salt
freshly ground pepper
½ bottle dry white wine
2 tablespoons butter

Method:

1. Peel and wash the vegetables. Place them at the bottom of a heavy, deep-sided roasting pan (preferably cast iron) with the unpeeled garlic cloves and the *bouquet garni*.
2. Open up the rib roast so that it lies flat on a board.
3. Remove most of the outer layer of fat from the kidney.
4. Sprinkle the surfaces of the veal with salt and pepper and place a few strips of kidney fat in the center;

then place the entire kidney on top.
5. Roll up the veal and tie with kitchen string.

6. Place the meat on top of the vegetables in the pan, add the wine, sprinkle with salt, and top with the butter cut into bits. Bake in a 350° oven for 2 hours.
7. Slice the roast, arrange on a platter, degrease the cooking juices, garnish with the vegetables, and serve.

My advice

It's easy to dice vegetables if you have a good knife that is neither too large nor too small, with a straight blade a little wider near the handle, and a sharp point.

To slice onions, peel them, cut them in half, and thinly slice each half.

To chop onions finely, cut them in half. Thinly slice each half horizontally without cutting through, then slice them vertically, again without cutting all the way through. Now, cut again horizontally all the way through; you will have a very fine

dice. With a little practice, this is a quick method, but watch out for your fingers. You may also use a food processor, but be careful—it works fast. Don't let it puree the onions.

Wine, butter, and cream are essential elements in cooking. Wine is particularly important in this veal roast. Don't skimp when you pour it. You should always use a good, dry white wine: good wine equals good cooking.

To make a successful veal roast, you should tie it tightly with kitchen string so that it keeps its shape and the stuffing doesn't escape. It would be even better to have your butcher roll and tie it for you, but remind him to season the inside of the veal with salt and pepper before rolling it around the kidney.

Don't forget to remove the string at serving time.

There are numerous ways of tying a roast so that it will keep its shape

while it is cooking. You can do it the butcher's way, by making your first tie around the middle of the meat, then at each quarter, then at intervals of about 2 inches. Finally, tie the string around the length of the roast, in the middle, and once on either side. Some butchers use elastic webbing to save time.

CHOCOLATE MOUSSE
Mousse au chocolat

Ingredients for 4 people:

8 tablespoons (1 stick) butter
7 ounces bitter (dark) chocolate, cut in
   small pieces
6 eggs, separated
⅔ cup sugar
⅓ cup very strong coffee

Method:

1. Melt the butter in a saucepan
over low heat, add the chocolate and
allow to melt, stirring constantly.
2. Place the egg yolks and sugar in
a bowl and beat with a whisk until
smooth and light colored.
3. Gradually add the coffee and
chocolate to the eggs. Mix well.

4. Beat the egg whites until stiff.
Add a small amount of egg whites to
the egg yolk mixture, then gently
fold the egg yolk mixture into the
egg whites.

5. Carefully pour the mousse into a
serving bowl. Chill overnight for
best results.

Farmer's cheese with herbs Lyon-style

This *fromage blanc frais* with herbs is an old Lyon recipe that has proved itself over the years. Called "silk weavers' brains" *(cervelle des canuts)*, this dish was made centuries ago by the silk weavers of Lyon and was often their main meal, eaten with boiled or baked potatoes. The farmer's cheese used here is made from cow's milk. Herbs are essential to this recipe, but they don't have to be those indicated. Furthermore, you may use more or less of one or another. The herbs should be fresh and not too finely chopped or they will lose their flavor.

This dish may be served as an hors d'oeuvre or at the end of the meal with other cheeses.

Breaded whiting English-style

This breaded fish is served with a *maître d'hôtel* butter. It is called "English-style," but to me it seems like a typically French dish.

You can also use another fish in place of the whiting in this recipe. Perch would be excellent prepared this way.

To make a genuine success of this dish, prepare the bread crumbs yourself with good-quality white bread. Use only the best butter (from Charentes or Normandy*) without a high water content, which causes the butter to burn when cooked. If you can't obtain imported butter, add a few drops of oil to the pan. This will prevent the butter from burning.

*EDITOR'S NOTE: Charentes or Normandy butter is available in some gourmet and specialty food shops. Or use a fresh, unsalted farm butter.

Apple fritters

A dessert loved by adults and children alike, apple fritters are easy to make. They should be served slightly warm and sprinkled with powdered sugar. In certain regions of France, they are accompanied by vanilla ice cream or fruit preserves.

You may peel the apples or leave their skin intact, according to your taste. If you are making this dessert for children, omit the rum and marinate the apples in lemon juice instead. The batter can be prepared with milk or water instead of beer, with the addition of a teaspoon of baking powder. For adults, the beer may be replaced by white wine. Choose the combination best suited to your individual taste.

FARMER'S CHEESE WITH HERBS LYON-STYLE

Fromage frais en salade à la lyonnaise

Ingredients for 4 people:

2½ cups fresh farmer's cheese
4 sprigs parsley
2 sprigs chives
2 sprigs chervil
2 sprigs tarragon
1 garlic clove
1 shallot
sea salt
freshly ground pepper
2–3 tablespoons olive oil
2–3 tablespoons white or red wine
   vinegar
1 cup *crème fraîche* or heavy cream

Method:

1. Put the farmer's cheese in a large bowl.

2. Pick through the herbs, remove the stems, rinse them quickly, and chop them coarsely.

3. Peel and finely chop the garlic and shallot.

4. Add the herbs to the cheese; add salt and pepper to taste, oil, and vinegar.

5. Finally, add the cream and beat with a whisk until well combined.

6. Allow to stand in the refrigerator for several hours before serving.

BREADED WHITING ENGLISH-STYLE
Merlans panés à l'anglaise

Ingredients for 4 people:

4 whitings (approximately ½ pound each)
sea salt
freshly ground pepper
4 eggs, beaten
1–2 cups bread crumbs
2 tablespoons butter

FOR THE SAUCE:

6 tablespoons butter
1–2 tablespoons chopped parsley
juice of 1 lemon

Method:

1. Cut open each fish along both sides of its dorsal spine and carefully remove the spine. Spread each side apart so the fish lies flat.

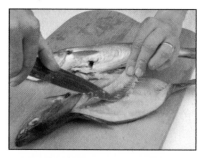

2. Sprinkle the fish with salt and pepper, dip in the beaten eggs, then in the bread crumbs.
3. In a large skillet, melt the butter and sauté the fish until golden, about 5 minutes on each side, beginning with the back.

4. Combine the remaining 6 tablespoons of butter, lemon juice, and parsley with a fork; add salt and pepper to taste.
5. Place a piece of flavored butter on each fish and serve while the butter slowly melts.

APPLE FRITTERS

Beignets aux pommes reinettes

Ingredients for 4 people:

4 Granny Smith or other tart apples
4 tablespoons rum

FOR THE BATTER:

½ cup flour
1 tablespoon sugar
pinch of sea salt
¾ cup beer
2 eggs
4 tablespoons butter
oil for frying
powdered sugar

Method:

1. Peel, core, and slice the apples into rounds. Place them on a plate, moisten with rum, and set aside to soak.
2. In a large bowl, combine flour, sugar, and salt.
3. Add the beer and the eggs and mix gently to obtain a smooth, thick batter.
4. Melt the butter and add to the batter.
5. Dip the apple slices into the bat-ter, then fry in very hot oil (360° F) until golden brown. Drain on paper towels.

6. Arrange on platter, sprinkle with powdered sugar, and serve.

My advice

Fish is of great importance in cooking. As we are almost entirely surrounded by the ocean, we are lucky enough to find very fresh fish in our markets and are eating more and more fish at home.

In some areas that are farther from the sea, frozen fish is used, but it is not on a par with fresh fish. There are countless fish recipes; here is just a sampling:

Poached fish

Place the cleaned, gutted fish on the rack of a fish poacher or shallow saucepan and pour over it a cold *court-bouillon*. Bring to a boil, then reduce the heat and simmer for 10 minutes. To make the *court-bouillon*, use white wine, vinegar, onions, celery, carrots, and parsley; for certain fish, such as turbot, cod, or haddock, you can use a mixture of water and milk instead of wine.

Season with cloves, bay leaves, peppercorns, and salt.

Fried fish

This way of cooking fish is particularly prized in the Mediterranean region of France.

Use a clean oil that is able to withstand high temperatures without burning. The best of these, in my opinion, is peanut oil. Small fish or cut-up fish is generally used when frying. The oil should be smoking when you add the fish, as it should cook through while it crisps on the outside. Keep an eye on the temperature of the oil.

Sautéed fish

Who is not familiar with this method? Sprinkle salt and pepper

over ready-to-cook fish and roll it in flour. Sauté the fish in a very hot mixture of butter and a small amount of oil. Sauté on top of the stove in a skillet, or in the oven in a heatproof dish, surrounded by a few unpeeled garlic cloves.

Braised fish

This method is generally used for large whole fish. Butter a baking dish large enough to hold the fish comfortably. Cover the bottom with cut-up vegetables: carrots, celery root, mushrooms, tomatoes, spring onions—all will do perfectly well. Place the fish, seasoned on all sides with salt and pepper, on top of the vegetables; moisten with white wine, red wine, or fish stock. Cover and cook in the oven, basting often. At high heat, the skin will take on a dark golden sheen. Remove the fish and reduce the sauce on top of the stove, if necessary.

Broiled fish

It is not easy to broil a very large fish; use smaller fish that cook quickly. As they broil, brush them often with oil or melted butter so that the skin becomes crisp. For large fish (over 4 pounds), make diagonal slits in the flesh on either side with a sharp knife. This will help the fish to cook evenly.

Today, commercially available electric grills are of high quality.

You can also place the fish on a sheet of wax paper in the oven and you will have a fish broiled with no fat. Simply brush lightly with a drop or two of oil.

Pumpkin soup

If you use an entire pumpkin you'll have a lot of soup, but you can use the pumpkin shell as a tureen, which will make a peasant soup look spectacular. Invite plenty of friends or make the soup as a first course when the entire family gets together on a Sunday or at Christmas. When the soup is finished, the pumpkin shell can be given to the children to make a jack-o'-lantern with a candle inside to light up the face.

To empty the pumpkin, cut a circular lid from the top and remove the flesh with a spoon, taking care not to break through the rind. Remove the seeds, which you can later plant or toast in the oven, to be served with cocktails.

Lamb chops with potatoes

This dish originated in the Savoie region of France. In the past, the dish was carried to the bakery and slid into the huge oven to cook. When the special Sunday bread was ready, so was the midday meal.

If, by chance, you do not wish to use lamb chops for this dish, you may use veal or even pork chops. Another tip: put in the garlic only after the liquid has been added; garlic fried in oil is traditional only in Italian cuisine.

Remove the meat from the refrigerator an hour before you are ready to cook. To enhance the flavor, rub your baking dish with a garlic clove.

Serve the dish on well-heated plates, as congealed lamb fat is unsavory. On the other hand, when the fat is very hot, it is delicious.

Grandmother Bocuse's waffles

Making waffles can be a party in itself, and when they arrive at the table, everyone is thrilled. These waffles are very rich, but you may prepare them with a little less butter and cream if you wish. A waffle iron is, of course, indispensable, and electric ones give very good results.

Don't worry if the first waffle doesn't come out right. A cook's proverb says that the first waffle is for the dog.

As the batter contains a great deal of butter, you don't have to butter the waffle iron; just brush it lightly with oil for the first waffle.

Sprinkled with powdered sugar and served very hot, these waffles are a real treat.

PUMPKIN SOUP
Soupe de courge

Ingredients for 4 people:

2 small leeks
5 tablespoons butter
1 pound pumpkin or squash meat
¾ pound potatoes
1 cup cold milk
1 cup cold water
sea salt
freshly ground pepper
⅓ cup *crème fraiche* or heavy cream

Method:

1. Peel, clean, and slice the leeks into 1-inch rounds and sauté them in butter in a saucepan. Do not allow them to brown.

2. Cut the pumpkin or squash and the potatoes into chunks and add to the leeks.

3. Add the milk and water, salt and pepper to taste, and cook over moderate heat for 30 minutes.

4. Puree the soup with a whisk or in a food processor, add the cream, and serve.

LAMB CHOPS WITH POTATOES

Côtes d'agneau aux pommes de terre

Ingredients for 4 people:

3 pound potatoes
1 large onion
3 tablespoons butter
4 thick, large lamb chops
sea salt
freshly ground pepper
1 sprig thyme
¼ bay leaf
3 cups cold water (approximately)
3 garlic cloves, finely chopped
a few small pieces of butter

Method:

1. Peel the potatoes and onion and slice. Sauté the onion in a skillet in 1 tablespoon of butter until golden.

2. Season the chops, potatoes, and onion with salt and pepper.

3. Sauté the chops in a skillet in 2 tablespoons of butter until brown.

4. Butter an ovenproof dish, place the thyme, bay leaf, and onions on the bottom.

5. Place the chops on the bed of onions and cover the chops with the potato slices.

6. Add the water, drop in the garlic, top with several pieces of butter,

and bake in a preheated 425° oven for 40 to 45 minutes.

GRANDMOTHER BOCUSE'S WAFFLES

Gaufres de Grand-mère Bocuse

Ingredients for 4 people:

1¼ cups flour
1 cup *crème fraîche* or heavy cream
1 tablespoon sugar
pinch of sea salt
1–2 tablespoons cold water
2 whole eggs
2 egg yolks
10 tablespoons butter
2 egg whites

TO SERVE:
apricot jam
powdered sugar

Method:

1. In a bowl, combine the flour, cream, sugar, salt, and water to obtain a smooth batter.
2. Add the whole eggs and egg yolks to the batter, as well as the softened butter.
3. Beat the egg whites into stiff peaks and fold them gently into the batter.

4. Cook the waffles in a hot, lightly greased waffle iron (about ¼ cup

batter per waffle).
5. Arrange the waffles on a serving dish, garnish with jam or sprinkle with powdered sugar.

My advice

Bouquet garni

The *bouquet garni* consists of herbs and vegetables tied together and used to flavor food.

For my *bouquet garni,* I use celery leaves, parsley, sprigs of thyme, a small bay leaf, and sometimes, depending on the dish, other aromatic herbs. The bundle is tied with strips of leek leaves so that it can be easily removed before the dish is served.

To peel tomatoes

Here's a little trick to peel tomatoes with ease. Cut a cross in the skin over the top of each tomato with a sharp knife and place it in boiling water for a few seconds.

Immediately hold it under cold running water. The skin will come off easily. Remove the stem end of the tomato only after peeling, or the water may penetrate the tomato and make it mushy.

The same method may be used to peel peaches and apricots.

Scrambled eggs with truffles

This dish should be prepared the day before it is to be served. You will need the best-quality ingredients: the freshest eggs, creamery butter. Utensils are important too: use a stainless steel, enamel, or ceramic saucepan (I prefer the last), a wooden spatula, and a stainless steel whisk or fork to avoid imparting a metallic taste to the eggs.

If you can't obtain fresh truffles, you can use canned; choose "peeled" or broken pieces rather than whole truffles as the former are less expensive.

You can also use white (or shiitake) mushrooms. Before adding them to the eggs, sauté them in a skillet so they release their water.

Remember to remove the egg-truffle mixture from the refrigerator at least an hour before cooking.

Coq au Vin

I always use a chicken from Bresse and a good bottle of wine for this dish. You surely know a recipe for *coq au vin*. Many variations exist for this most essential dish in the basic repertoire of French cuisine.

I bind the sauce from the *coq au vin* with the liver, heart, and blood of the poultry. If you are unable to find poultry blood, you may use pork blood instead, which your butcher should be able to give you. If blood is unavailable, bind the sauce by the method described on page 43.

A roaster or even a frying chicken may be used in place of poultry from Bresse, as long as the wine is good. A Burgundy is preferable; use a Pommard or a Châteauneuf du Pape. Serve the *coq au vin* with rice or fresh noodles.

Baked apples

This is a marvelous, easy-to-make dessert. A favorite with young and old alike, it requires few ingredients. The quality of the apples, however, is important to its success. Use Granny Smith apples, if available. After rinsing them well, wipe them carefully with a clean towel.

SCRAMBLED EGGS WITH TRUFFLES
Oeufs brouillés aux truffes

Ingredients for 4 people:

8 eggs
sea salt
freshly ground pepper
3½ ounces fresh truffles (or white or
  shiitake mushrooms, about 2 or 3,
  lightly sautéed)
2 tablespoons butter
1–2 tablespoons *crème fraiche* or
  heavy cream
    thin slices of truffle for garnish
      (or use fresh mushrooms)

Method:

1. Break the eggs into a bowl, add salt and pepper, and beat gently with a fork or small whisk.
2. Carefully peel the truffles and cut into small cubes.

3. Add the truffles to the egg mixture, cover, and refrigerate overnight.

4. Place the butter in a heat-resistant dish and place the dish in a *bain-marie*.
5. Pour the egg mixture into the dish and cook gently over low heat,

stirring constantly.
6. Add the *crème fraiche*, mix gently, adjust the seasoning, and divide the scrambled eggs among 4 small plates.
7. Garnish with the truffle slices and serve.

COQ AU VIN
Coq au vin

Ingredients for 4 people:

1 lean young stewing hen or roaster
   weighing about 4 to 4½ pounds
sea salt
freshly ground pepper
4 tablespoons butter
¼ pound bacon in one piece
1 small leek
1 bunch spring onions
2 carrots
2–3 garlic cloves, chopped
a few sprigs parsley
1 sprig fresh thyme
½ bay leaf
1 celery stalk
1 bottle good red wine
¼ pound sliced mushrooms or
   wild mushrooms
1 chicken liver
1 tablespoon flour
4 tablespoons cognac
2–3 tablespoons chopped parsley

Method:

1. Cut up the chicken, following directions on page 68.
2. Season the pieces with salt and pepper, and in an ovenproof casserole, brown gently in butter until golden.
3. Cut the bacon into small cubes, add to the casserole, and brown.

4. Peel the spring onions, leek, and carrots and cut into small chunks.
5. Add them to the chicken with the chopped garlic, herbs, and celery; add the wine.
6. Simmer for 30 to 40 minutes
7. Remove the vegetables and the choice pieces of chicken, except for the back, and arrange on a heated platter.
8. Add the mushrooms to the casserole (with the sauce and back) and

cook until just tender. Remove the mushrooms and add to the platter.
9. Mix the liver, finely chopped, and the flour and add to the sauce to thicken. Add the cognac.

10. Pour the sauce through a fine sieve over the platter of chicken and vegetables.
11. Sprinkle with parsley and serve.

BAKED APPLES
Pommes Bonne Femme

Ingredients for 4 people:

4 large baking apples
3 tablespoons butter
⅓ cup cold water
4 tablespoons sugar
4 tablespoons raspberry or
   red currant jelly

Method:

1. Wash and core the apples; split the skin in a circle around the middle of each apple so it doesn't burst.

2. Butter a baking dish and place the apples in it.
3. Place a nugget of butter in the hollowed core of each apple, pour the water over the apples, and sprinkle each of them with sugar.
4. Bake in a preheated 350° oven for 25–30 minutes.
5. Place a tablespoon of jelly in the core of each apple and serve very hot.

My advice

Fresh herbs are essential to today's cooking. If they are not available on a daily basis at the market, you can plant an herb garden in your yard or grow them in pots on your windowsill.

Freeze-dried or frozen herbs available commercially are useful alternatives to fresh herbs, but will not give you the same delicious flavor.

The following is a short list of the most important herbs, those that you should always have on hand and that will heighten the taste of your cooking.

Basil

Fresh basil leaves are delicious in soups, tomato sauces, meat, fish, and poultry dishes, as well as in vegetables and salads. Add some to your pasta just before serving.

Chervil

Only the delicate fresh leaves of this herb should be used. It complements perfectly potato and herb soups, salads, sauces, and herb butters, and heightens the flavor of omelettes.

Dill

This rather strongly flavored herb is generally used with delicate foods. It is especially good with fish and vegetables, but also with lamb, veal, and poultry, as well as salads, egg-based dishes, soups, and certain sauces.

Parsley

At home in every sort of cuisine, parsley has a variety of uses. Freshly chopped, it should be added just before the end of cooking, in order to enliven the flavor and appearance of the dish.

Rosemary

This herb should be used in moderation, as its flavor is intensely aromatic. It goes well with lamb, goose, duck, and game, or blended into aromatic oils and marinades.

Sage

This herb compliments pork and veal. Like rosemary, it should be used in small doses, as its flavor is strong.

Savory

The flavor of savory is intense, so use discretion when adding it to your dishes. It goes well in any bean recipe, in *potées* (boiled dinners), in hearty soups, and in lamb dishes and hashes.

Tarragon

This herb with its fine flavor is used in sauces, soups, and salads, as well as with fish, poultry, and veal and in egg dishes.

Thyme

Thyme can be used with all hearty foods—game, pork, beef, boiled dinners—and in *court-bouillon*.

Gilthead in white wine

Cooking with wine doesn't mean adding alcohol to your dishes, for the alcohol evaporates when the wine boils and the wine becomes a flavoring. The proof: at the restaurant I share with Roger Vergé and Gaston Lenôtre in Disney World's Epcot Center, in Florida, the childrens' meal is *boeuf bourguignon.*

I chose a gilthead for the first course, but you may use another sort of fish. Red snapper, carp, pike, and perch are all fine substitutes; even mullet would do nicely. The important thing is to choose a firm-fleshed fish of the proper size. For 4 people, count 3 to 3½ pounds of fish.

Have your fishmonger clean and prepare the fish or, if you wish, do it yourself. Scaly fish need to be scaled, gutted like any other, and well cleaned.

Boeuf bourguignon

Beef stewed slowly in Burgundy wine is a dish famous in that wine region of France. This does not mean that you must use a Burgundy, as long as the wine you choose is a good one.

Neither should you limit yourself to beef; this dish can be just as delicate and flavorful with other kinds of meats, such as pork. The procedure and other ingredients remain the same whatever meat and wine you choose. You may use rabbit as well. In that case, it would be called *lapin en civet,* rabbit stew, and the sauce would be thickened with the animal's blood.

To enliven the dish, try adding a handful of mushrooms a few moments before serving.

Poached pears in wine

This is yet another dish in which I use a great deal of red wine. In this case, a Beaujolais is a good choice— for instance a Saint-Amour—or even a Burgundy. As with all recipes using wine, don't skimp on it.

The pears, the stars of this recipe, should remain firm after cooking and not disintegrate. I like to use small, slightly green pears or *passe-crassane* (a Comice type of pear).

You will see that it is an excellent dessert with an eye-catching color and a perfume that pervades the house during its preparation.

GILTHEAD IN WHITE WINE
Daurade au vin blanc

Ingredients for 4 people:

3 tablespoons butter
4 shallots, finely chopped
¼ pound sliced fresh mushrooms
4 tomatoes, peeled, seeded, and coarsely
   chopped
1 small bay leaf
1 sprig thyme
1 sprig tarragon
1 bunch parsley, chopped
1 gilthead, about 3 pounds
sea salt
freshly ground pepper
½ bottle dry white wine
several small pieces of butter

Method:

1. Butter an ovenproof dish and place in it the shallots, mushrooms, tomatoes, and the herbs, cleaned and chopped.

2. Season the cavity of the fish with salt and place it on top of the vegetable-herb mixture. Sprinkle with salt and pepper and pour the wine over it.

3. Place a few bits of butter on top,

cover with a sheet of aluminum foil, and bake for about 30 minutes in a preheated 400° oven.

4. Remove from the oven and serve immediately.

BOEUF BOURGUIGNON
Boeuf bourguignon

Ingredients for 4 people:

2 pounds beef chuck
¼ pound smoked bacon in one piece
sea salt
freshly ground pepper
¾ pound carrots
1 bunch spring onions
4 tablespoons butter
2 tablespoons flour
5 tablespoons cognac
1 bottle red Burgundy wine
2 garlic cloves
1 *bouquet garni*

Method:

1. Cut the chuck and bacon into chunks, season with salt (not too much, as the bacon is already salty) and pepper.
2. Peel and cut the vegetables into chunks.
3. Heat the butter in a casserole or stew pot, sauté the bacon, and then brown the beef. Add the vegetables and sauté gently.
4. Sprinkle the flour on the meat,

deglaze* with the cognac, and lastly add the wine.
5. Add the garlic cloves, thinly sliced, and the *bouquet garni,* cover and simmer the stew for 1½ to 2½ hours, depending on the quantity of meat used.

*EDITOR'S NOTE: To deglaze, skim off as much fat as possible from casserole, add cognac, and ignite quickly to burn off any remaining fat.

POACHED PEARS IN WINE
Poires au vin rouge

Ingredients for 4 people:

8 small or 4 large pears
¼ pound sugar lumps
1 stick cinnamon
2 vanilla beans
2 cloves
5 peppercorns
2–3 tablespoons red currant jelly
1 bottle red wine

Method:

1. Peel the pears and place them in a small saucepan, stem up.

2. Add the sugar, spices, and jelly, then pour in the wine. Cook them over medium heat; they should be done in about 20 minutes.

3. Arrange the pears in a dessert bowl, pour the spiced wine over them, chill, and serve.

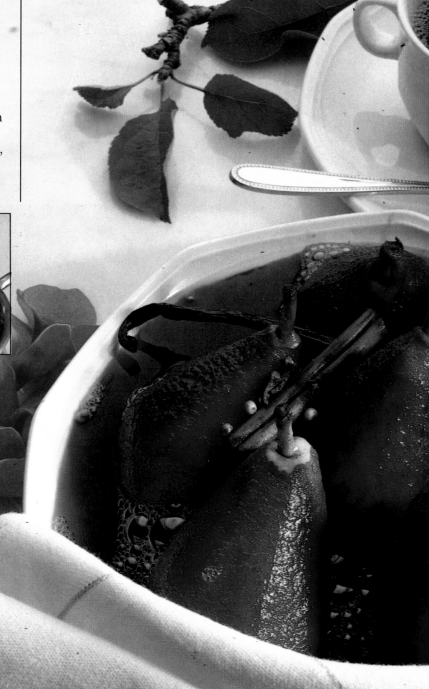

My advice

It isn't absolutely necessary to offer a different wine with each course; in fact, your meal can be just as delightful accompanied by a single red or white wine. White wine is usually served with fish, a Saint-Véran or a Mâcon, for example; with a more refined dish, a Pouilly-Fuissé. The choice is large and even more so when choosing red wine. To mention only a few, you can accompany an entire three-course meal with a Beaujolais—a Morgon, Saint-Amour, or Chiroubles—or, for a festive meal, a Burgundy or Bordeaux.

Let's now look at a few important rules that apply to the manner in which wine is served.

It is true that rules are made to be broken, but nevertheless we should remember several points: white wine is served before red, young wine before old, lighter wines before those with more body, and finally, dry wines before sweet.

Temperature is vital to the full appreciation of wine. White wine should be served between 45° and 50°F, a light red wine between 50° and 57°, and a hearty or old red between 57° and 64°. Another basic rule is to avoid serving wine with dishes and salads made with vinegar. Wines don't go well with fruit or chocolate desserts either; it is better to drink water.

The storage of wine plays an important part in the quality of the wine you enjoy. Here are three rules of thumb for maintaining a wine cellar:

1. The wines should be kept in a dark place. Light causes the wine to mature too quickly and has a negative effect on its bouquet.
2. The bottles should be stored on their sides. The wine stays in contact with the cork, which then does not dry out; furthermore, air cannot get into the bottle.
3. The ideal temperature for storing wine is between 46° and 57°F.

A wine-tasting session with my friend Georges Dubœuf at Romanèche-Thorins.

Soup with truffles Elysée

I recreated this recipe in 1975 for
Valéry Giscard d'Estaing, then the
president of France, to commemo-
rate being awarded the cross of the
Légion d'Honneur, but this truffle
soup is actually a traditional dish
popular in the Ardèche region of
France. It is a soup for special occa-
sions, as its ingredients are rather
costly.

I use truffles from Périgord, unpeeled so as to fully retain their
aroma and taste. I cook the soup in
individual soup bowls with feet; the
soup simmers gently since it does
not sit directly on the bottom of the
oven.

Steak with wine sauce

The wine sauce for this dish is prepared with a Beaujolais. The steak
should be well-aged beef. It should
be removed from the refrigerator at
least 2 to 3 hours before preparation
so that it is at room temperature.
The wine drunk during the meal
should be the same Beaujolais used
in the sauce.

As an accompaniment, I recom-
mend noodles, rice, mashed
potatoes, or spinach puree.

Crêpes with orange marmalad

Now I will reveal the secret of the
orange crêpes the way we used to
prepare them at Fernand Point's. It
is a rich recipe, which I prefer to prepare with just a sprinkling of sugar,
but you may wish to add a few drops
of cognac or Grand Marnier.

These crêpes are truly delicious
when they are very thin. Cook them
in a small skillet or crêpe pan over
moderate heat.

SOUP WITH TRUFFLES ELYSÉE
Soupe aux truffes Elysée

Ingredients for 4 people:

4 tablespoons Noilly Prat or other
   dry vermouth
3 cups strong chicken consommé
4 fresh black truffles (canned truffles
   can be used)
½ pound canned *foie gras*
1 cup of a mixture of carrots, onions,
   celery, and mushrooms finely diced
   and gently sautéed in butter
3½ ounces cooked chicken breast
sea salt
freshly ground pepper
2 egg yolks, beaten

4 rounds of puff or flaky pastry about 6
   inches in diameter

Method:

1. Divide the vermouth and the
consommé among 4 individual heat-
resistant soup bowls.
2. Add the truffles, sliced thin, the
foie gras, cut into small pieces, the
vegetable mixture, and the chicken
breast, also finely sliced. Add salt
and pepper to taste.

3. Place a pastry round on top of
each bowl and seal the sides firmly
so that the soup's flavor is trapped
within.

4. Brush the pastry with the
beaten egg yolk and bake the soup
in a preheated 425° oven for 18 to 20
minutes. Serve.

STEAK WITH WINE SAUCE
Entrecôte vigneronne

Ingredients for 4 people:

2 rib steaks each weighing about
   1¼ pounds
sea salt
freshly ground pepper
¼ pound shallots, chopped
1 teaspoon flour
1 bottle Beaujolais red wine
⅓ cup chopped parsley

Method:

1. Season the meat with salt and pepper. Melt half the butter in a skillet and brown the meat for about 7 or 8 minutes on each side. Set aside and keep hot.

2. In the same butter, gently sauté the shallots, sprinkle them with flour, add the wine, and reduce until the sauce has thickened.

3. Add pepper to taste, add the rest of the butter to the sauce, and bring to a boil, stirring constantly.

4. Add the parsley and adjust the seasoning.

5. Pour the sauce over the steaks and serve.

CRÊPES WITH ORANGE MARMALADE
Crêpes à l'orange

Ingredients for 4 people:

FOR THE BATTER:

½ cup flour
1 tablespoon sugar
pinch of sea salt
1 cup cold milk
2 eggs
9 tablespoons butter, melted

TO SERVE:

bitter orange marmalade
powdered sugar

Method:

1. In a bowl, combine the flour, sugar, and salt.

2. Add the milk gradually, then the eggs, and finally the melted butter and beat with a whisk to obtain a smooth batter.

3. Make the crêpes by pouring a couple of tablespoons of batter into an ungreased heated crêpe pan. Cook on both sides.

4. Spread a little marmalade on each crêpe, fold in half, and sprinkle with powdered sugar.

Beef

To get good beef, you need a good butcher, one you can trust. The meat he gives you will be tender because it has aged from 2 to 4 weeks "on the bone." Generally, well-marbled meats are tastier and age better than very lean meats.

After you have purchased your cut of meat, boned and ready to cook, do not keep it more than a day or two. Your refrigerator is not designed to keep meat for long periods.

Wrap it well in plastic wrap (but not in aluminum foil), so that it doesn't absorb odors from melon, other fruit, or cheese.

Here are the different types of beef from the first category, those used for roasting or broiling.

International Vocabulary		
French	*English*	*German*
bleu	rare	innen roh-blau
saignant	medium rare	innen vollrot-blutig
anglais	underdone	voll rosa-rosa
à point	medium	in Kern rosa-halbrosa
bien cuit	well done	innen grau-durch

2. A **chateaubriand** is a slice from the best part of the heart of the whole filet, about 1 to 1½ inches

thick. There are two to a filet. The following cuts differ only in thickness.

3. Steaks or **filets mignons** are cut across the grain about ⅔ to ¾ of an inch thick.

4. Tournedos are thicker, about ¾ to 1 inch, and are cut across the grain from the last third of the filet.

5. The **tail of the filet** can either be cut with the grain into slices ¾ of an inch thick or into small cubes to be simply sautéed.

6. A **rib roast** on the bone, serving 6 to 8 people and oven roasted, is to me the tastiest cut.

7. For a good **roast beef,** count 15 minutes per pound in a 375° oven, but only if the meat has been removed from the refrigerator at least 4 hours before cooking.

1. The **filet,** the tenderest and most popular cut, weighs 6½ to 7 ounces whole and should be cut across the grain in slices ¾ to 1 inch thick.

Mackerel in white wine

It is always surprising to discover that the most delicious dishes can be prepared with the simplest of ingredients.

Fish cooked with white wine belongs to a family of simple, easy-to-prepare dishes that are immensely pleasing to the taste buds. Fresh mackerel can be found in most fish markets; however, other fish are also delicious prepared in this way. Whether it is salt-water or fresh-water fish, it is only their taste or what is available in the market that determines the recipe.

If you've been fishing, by all means use this recipe for your own catch. You can use a little gadget called a "fluter" to cut up the carrots; the slices then look like little flowers and dress up this simple dish.

Poached chicken

This is a very old dish that my grandparents used to serve with great success at their inn. Traditionally, it was called "hen in a shirt." As the poultry cooks in its own juice inside the pork bladder (or roasting bag),* it takes on a wonderful flavor, even better with the addition of vegetables and truffles.

It is important to use a scrupulously clean pork bladder, and it should be softened by soaking in water overnight. Then it should be turned inside out.

*EDITOR'S NOTE: As pork bladders are not commonly available in the United States, a roasting bag makes an excellent substitute.

Souffléed omelette

I lighten this sweet omelette by beating the egg whites separately. To stiffen them, add a pinch of salt, which prevents graininess and helps the egg whites to become smooth. Do not stir, but fold the other mixture gently into the egg whites with a rubber or wooden spatula. Of course, you can beat the egg whites in a food processor or with an electric egg beater, but I prefer using a stainless steel whisk and a copper bowl; it isn't the least bit more difficult.

MACKEREL IN WHITE WINE
Maquereaux au vin blanc

Ingredients for 4 people:

- 4 mackerel, gutted and cleaned
- 4 spring onions
- 1 shallot
- 1 carrot
- 1 celery stalk
- 1 sprig tarragon
- 1 sprig thyme
- 1 sprig parsley
- 1 sprig chervil
- 1/4 bay leaf
- 3 cloves
- 1/4 bottle white wine (about 1 cup)
- 1 cup wine vinegar
- 1 cup cold water
- sea salt
- freshly ground pepper

Method:

1. Arrange the mackerel in a baking dish.

2. Peel and thinly slice the spring onions and shallot.

3. Scrape the carrot and thinly slice into rounds or sticks.

4. Place the vegetables, herbs, and cloves in a saucepan.

5. Add the wine, vinegar, water, and salt and pepper to taste. This mixture of liquid and vegetables is called a *nage* (bath) in the French culinary vocabulary.

6. Boil for 15 minutes over moderate heat.

7. Pour the boiling liquid and vegetables over the mackerel, place them in a preheated 425° oven for 15 minutes, and serve.

POACHED CHICKEN
Poularde en vessie

Ingredients for 4 people:

1 chicken, about 4 pounds
1 large truffle, fresh or canned

FOR THE STUFFING:

1½ ounces fresh peas
1½ ounces canned corn
1½ ounces string beans
1½ ounces carrots
1½ ounces canned or frozen artichoke
  hearts
½ sweetbread
1½ ounces canned *foie gras*
¼ cup raw rice
1½ ounces mushrooms
sea salt
freshly ground pepper
plastic roasting bag

Method:

1. Slice half the truffle thinly and slide the slices underneath the breast skin of the chicken, taking care not to cut or tear the skin.

2. Clean the vegetables, and where necessary, cut them into small pieces. Cook them in boiling salted water for 8 to 10 minutes.
3. Drain the vegetables and set aside.
4. Cook the rice in water or broth 15 to 18 minutes or until just tender.
5. Cut the sweetbread and *foie gras* into small pieces, add them to the rice, mushrooms, and the rest of the truffle cut in small pieces.
6. Combine thoroughly the vegeta-ble mixture and the rice–*foie gras* mixture. Season with salt and pepper to taste.

7. Fill the cavity of the chicken with the stuffing, seal, and tie with kitchen string.

8. Place the chicken in the roasting bag and immerse in a large pot of cold water. Simmer for 1½ hours. Open the bag, carve the bird, and serve each piece surrounded by some of the stuffing.

SOUFFLÉED OMELETTE
Omelette soufflée

Ingredients for 4 people:

8 egg yolks
4 tablespoons brown sugar
1 vanilla bean
8 egg whites
pinch of sea salt
1½ ounces rum
approximately 6 tablespoons butter

TO SERVE:
apricot preserves
powdered sugar

Method:

1. In a large bowl, beat together the egg yolks, the brown sugar, and the scrapings from the inside of the vanilla bean.

2. Beat the egg whites with a pinch of salt until stiff.

3. Carefully fold the yolk mixture into the beaten egg whites.

4. Add the rum. Melt the butter in a round baking dish and pour in the batter.

5. Bake in a preheated 350° oven for 10 to 15 minutes, or until puffed and golden.

6. Remove from the oven, slide onto a serving dish, and split the omelette down the middle.

7. Put some apricot preserves in the center, fold over, sprinkle with powdered sugar, and serve.

My advice

A wide variety of spices is necessary for good cooking. They should always be stored in a dark place in well-sealed jars so that they don't lose their flavor. If at all possible, add only freshly ground spices to your dishes. Whole seeds, grains, and leaves can be cooked along with the food. Remove them before serving, as it can be very unpleasant to feel a juniper berry, for instance, cracking between your teeth.

Cinnamon

Cinnamon is a dark golden spice usually in powdered form. It has a pleasant, smooth, warm aroma that goes well with sweet dishes in general: apple tarts, pears in wine, chocolate, vanilla.

Coriander

Coriander plays an important role in curry. It is also used in the preparation of soups, meats, and cauliflower, as well as certain marinades and vegetables *à la grecque* (marinated).

Curry

Curry powder is now considered to be a spice in its own right, although it is really a mixture of spices that can vary considerably. The most common type of powder includes turmeric, cardamom, nutmeg, cloves, cinnamon, star anise, coriander, caraway, ginger, pepper, tangerine zest, fennel, and sesame seeds. Curry powder flavors rice and Indian-style cooking.

Fennel seed

Like aniseed, which it resembles, fennel is used mainly in fish dishes, usually grilled. It gives a distinctive taste to string beans, fava beans, and chick peas.

Mustard

There are about thirty types of this condiment, all flavored differently. But to me the only one true mustard is strong Dijon mustard.

Nutmeg

Two different types of this spice are used in cooking: whole nutmeg and mace. Each has an intense flavor and enhances white sauces, mashed potatoes and purees, creamy stews, potato and cauliflower *au gratin,* and certain cheese dishes.

Paprika

This spice is made mainly from red peppers. The ripe peppers are dried and ground. Depending on the type used, the spice can be hot or mild. Paprika is used to flavor stews and stuffings.

Pepper

To my mind, the best black pepper comes from Peru. I never use white pepper or ground pepper; only whole peppercorns, ground at the last moment. Unlike all other spices, pepper, if kept away from sources of light, improves with age.

Saffron

Its aromatic flavor and perfume make this one of the most sought-after spices in spite of its high cost. Saffron tints food a lovely golden-yellow and brings a wonderful warm taste to bouillabaisse and paella.

Salt

If you are as fussy as I am, you will use only sea salt.

Snails Burgundy-style

For this savory appetizer, you will need those delicious vine-fed snails from Burgundy. Unfortunately, I must tell you that they are slowly disappearing. If you are going to gather your own snails, be aware of the legal limitations in your area. Snails must be prepared before cooking, a rather difficult, time-consuming process, but you can use ready-to-use canned or frozen snails, which are just as good.

To make sure the snail butter is as green as possible, I salt the parsley, which then renders its juices and tints the butter.

Hunter's chicken

I use a chicken from Bresse for this recipe. Only chickens raised in this region carry its name. The chicken farmers there observe strict rules.

The Bresse chicken is recognizable by its bluish feet, white neck feathers, and red crest. Each bird sports a special tag. In the United States, use free-range chickens, which are very tasty and quite different from ordinary chickens.

Strawberry tart

This is a simple but delicious tart. What is important is the strawberries that garnish it. When buying them, choose berries that are bright red, ripe, sweet, and fruity.

The sweet dough of the recipe given here works particularly well with this dessert. It uses one part butter to two parts flour. Other fruit may also be used for the filling: raspberries, blackberries, blueberries, or even mangos, if you like exotic fruit. If you wish, you can also divide the dough in four and make four individual tartlets.

A little trick: to roll out the dough evenly, hold the rolling pin at its ends rather than toward the center. Place a round of wax paper on the bottom of the pan, so the crust doesn't stick when baked.

SNAILS BURGUNDY-STYLE
Escargots à la bourguignonne

Ingredients for 4 people:

4–5 sprigs parsley
1 shallot
1 garlic clove
3 tablespoons slivered almonds
1 teaspoon sea salt
10 tablespoons butter
freshly ground pepper
4 dozen canned French snails with shells

Method:

1. Finely chop the parsley, shallot, garlic, and almonds and mix together with the salt.
2. Cream the butter with a fork, add the above mixture and plenty of pepper to taste.
3. Place the snails in their shells and stuff each with some of the herb butter to seal.
4. Cook over low heat for 5-10 minutes; the butter should not

brown. Or bake the snails in a 425° oven for the same length of time. Remove from heat and serve immediately.

HUNTER'S CHICKEN
Poulet chasseur

Ingredients for 4 people:

1 chicken, about 4 pounds
  (free-range, preferably)
sea salt
freshly ground pepper
2 shallots
⅓ pound mushrooms
4 tomatoes, peeled and halved
½ bay leaf
a few sprigs tarragon
1 sprig thyme
1 small bunch parsley
3 tablespoons olive oil
2 garlic cloves
a few celery leaves
1 cup white wine

Method:

1. Cut up the chicken into serving-size pieces and season with salt and pepper.

2. Peel the shallots, clean the mushrooms, and combine with the tomatoes and herbs.
3. Heat the oil in a stew pot and lightly brown the chicken on all sides.
4. Add the garlic, celery leaves, white wine, and the tomato-mushroom mixture.
5. Allow to cook uncovered over moderate heat for half an hour.
6. Remove the pieces of chicken, set them aside and keep warm, and

reduce the sauce for about 10 minutes over high heat.
7. Pour the sauce over the chicken and serve.

With my team in the kitchen. Note that we use only copper pans for cooking.

My advice

If fresh snails are to be used, they must be starved for several days to empty their intestines of grass residue and other impurities. Wash them very well to remove all traces of mucus. Put them in boiling salted water and cook for 5 to 8 minutes. Rinse under running water and remove from the shells. Remove the black tip from each snail. Place the snails in a saucepan with equal amounts of white wine and water to cover, some diced vegetables, and a few sprigs of fresh herbs, and simmer gently for at least 3 hours. Drain.

To make a good hunter's chicken, or the famous *coq au vin,* you must cut up the poultry correctly.

To do this, hold each leg, one at a time, in your hand and pull it away from the body, then cut at the joint and remove the wing tips. Cut the breast and carcass into 3 pieces (2 breast pieces and the back). The back near the tail is, in my opinion, the tastiest part of the chicken. For

where the thigh meets the body. Now cut the wings at their joints

hunter's chicken, cut each piece in two; the thigh is cut away from the drumstick at the joint.

STRAWBERRY TART
Tarte aux fraises

Ingredients for 4 people:

FOR THE PASTRY:

⅓ cup sugar
1 cup flour
pinch of sea salt
4 tablespoons butter
1 whole egg
1 egg yolk
1–2 tablespoons cold water

FOR THE FILLING:

⅓ cup red currant jelly
2 pounds ripe strawberries
a few pistachio nuts, chopped

Method:

1. In a bowl, combine the sugar, flour, and salt.
2. Add the butter and work together with your hands.
3. Add the whole egg, the egg yolk, and the water and combine until a smooth dough is obtained.
4. Form a ball with the dough and allow to rest for an hour.

5. Roll it out on a floured surface to form a round slightly larger than your tart pan, then slide onto the pan.
6. Bake for 20 to 25 minutes in a 350° oven.
7. Remove from oven and brush the pastry with half of the jelly.

8. Arrange the strawberries on top of the jelly and brush them with the rest of it, gently heated. Scatter the chopped pistachios over the tart and serve.

Cream of asparagus soup

For this soup, use small, green, fresh asparagus. Any other type of asparagus will do, even white asparagus, but you won't end up with as beautiful a color. Use whatever kind is available, but make sure it is fresh and of the best quality. A few asparagus tips, blanched in boiling salted water for 5 to 10 minutes, should be reserved for garnish. This is true of any vegetables used for decoration. Prepared this way, they retain their firmness and full flavor.

Old-fashioned veal stew

To make this stew the way our grandmothers did, you need three different cuts of veal: the shoulder, the breast, and the neck, all very juicy. You can use other cuts, but what is important here is the combination of different textures: one should be slightly gelatinous, another a bit chewy, and the third quite meaty to give plenty of flavor to the stew.

Veal stew prepared in this manner will have a delicious sauce. To thicken it, I use a mixture of cream and egg yolk. Add it to the sauce at the very last moment and turn off the heat immediately or the egg will coagulate and give the sauce an unpleasant appearance. If this dish is successful, it will charm everyone at the table.

Crème brûlée

This is an old family recipe. Children adore it and adults say it's divine.

The ingredients are easy to find and quite inexpensive. Excellent dishes can be prepared with simple ingredients; you don't always have to use lobster, caviar, or truffles. I repeat here that it's the freshness of the ingredients, and not their price, that constitutes the basis of good cooking.

In this recipe, the important ingredient is brown sugar or unrefined cane sugar. It gives a very special flavor to this dessert. The cream used here is whipping cream.

CREAM OF ASPARAGUS SOUP
Crème d'asperges

Ingredients for 4 people:

1 pound asparagus
¼ pound potatoes
2 small leeks
4 tablespoons butter
sea salt
1 cup cold milk
1 cup cold water
3 tablespoons *crème fraiche* or
    heavy cream
1 large pat of butter
freshly ground pepper

Method:

1. Peel the asparagus stalks and cut them into little pieces, reserving a few whole tips for garnish.

2. Peel the potatoes and cut into small cubes. They thicken and bind the soup.

3. Peel and wash the leeks, slice them crosswise, and sauté them gently in butter in a large saucepan. Season with salt to taste. The leeks intensify the flavor of the soup.

4. Add the asparagus and potatoes and briefly sauté. Add the water and milk and simmer for about 20 minutes.

5. Remove from heat, allow to rest briefly; meanwhile, blanch the reserved tips and rinse under cold water.

6. Puree the soup in a food processor or blender, or puree by hand.

7. Add the *crème fraîche* and the pat of butter, season with pepper to taste, and stir gently.

8. Pour the soup into a serving bowl, garnish with the asparagus tips, and serve.

OLD-FASHIONED VEAL STEW
Blanquette de veau à l'ancienne

Ingredients for 4 people:

¾ pound breast of veal
¾ pound shoulder of veal
¾ pound veal neck
sea salt
freshly ground pepper
4 tablespoons butter
2–3 carrots
4 small onions
1 celery stalk
1 sprig thyme
¼ bay leaf
a few sprigs parsley
1 garlic clove
1–2 cloves
1 tablespoon flour
1 cup white wine
1–2 cups cold water
¾ pound mushrooms
2 egg yolks
⅓ cup *crème fraîche* or heavy cream

To serve:
2–3 tablespoons chopped parsley

Method:

1. Cut the meat into chunks, season with salt and pepper, and in a large stew pot, brown the meat lightly in the butter.
2. Add the carrots, peeled and cut into large pieces, the onions and garlic, peeled, and the herbs and spices. Braise briefly, uncovered.

3. Sprinkle the meat with the flour, add the wine and water.

4. Bring to a boil, skim lightly, cover, and simmer gently for an hour.
5. Remove the meat and vegetables, place them in another pot, pass the sauce through a sieve over the meat, add the mushrooms, whole, and cook for 5 minutes more.
6. Add pepper to taste and remove from heat.

7. Beat the cream and egg yolks together and stir into the stew.
8. Arrange the stew on a platter, sprinkle with chopped parsley, and serve.

CRÈME BRÛLÉE
Crème brûlée

Ingredients for 4 people:

⅔ cup brown sugar
1 vanilla bean
4 egg yolks
1½ cups cold milk
1 cup heavy cream

Method:

1. Split the vanilla bean, scrape the inside, and add the scrapings to the sugar.

2. In a bowl, combine the egg yolks, sugar, and vanilla.

3. Add the milk and cream; mix well.

4. Pour the mixture into 4 individual ovenproof bowls. Bake in a preheated 300° oven for about 1 hour.

5. Sprinkle each custard with brown sugar, pass under the broiler until browned and slightly crusty, and serve lukewarm.

Beaujolais

The Beaujolais wines of France can be divided into three groups:

The Beaujolais that is produced in the southern part of Villefranche-sur-Saône, in the "Pierres Dorées" (Golden Rocks) country, where production is limited to about 3,000 liters an acre.

Beaujolais-Villages, which is produced in thirty different municipalities and is meant to be drunk while still young and fresh. It's the perfect "drinking" wine, a wine of great class available to everyone. Depending on its origins, it can satisfy the most demanding connoisseur and accompany many varied dishes.

Finally, the nine vintages: Saint-Amour, Juliénas, Chénas, Moulin-à-vent, Fleurie, Chiroubles, Morgon, Côte de Brouilly, Brouilly. Each has its own character; the most robust among them age well.

There's a fourth group, too: Beaujolais Nouveau. People the world over enjoy Beaujolais Nouveau, starting on the third Thursday of November each year. It's the big event of the year.

It is obvious that Beaujolais is a great wine, even when very young. Age has nothing to do with its quality.

Peas French-style

This is truly a springtime dish. Young lettuce and spring peas lend this recipe a subtle note. In the spring, fresh peas are so tender that once you have shelled them, you can cook the pods after removing their strings. One of the secrets behind the exquisite flavor of this dish is that the vegetables cook in their own juices. Prepare the vegetables the day before by seasoning them with salt, sugar, and pepper, so that their juices are rendered. Put them in the refrigerator. You can then cook them the next day in their own juices.

It is important to follow the directions exactly so that the flavor of the juice is not lost. Put cold water or ice cubes in a dish on top of the saucepan; the steam released while cooking will touch the cold plate and fall back onto the peas.

Eel stew

This recipe, which is part of the rich culinary tradition of river navigators, is also a specialty of the Saône region. The eel is simmered in a tasty Burgundy sauce.

Have your fishmonger prepare the eel for you, as the skinning of the fish demands a little practice.* If you wish to try it, slit the skin around the neck with a sharp knife and pull it back with pliers. This is difficult, as you must practically pull the skin back on itself. The rest is easy. Pull the skin off the eel, gut it, and for this recipe, cut it into pieces about 2 inches long. Do not add the garlic before the liquid.

*EDITOR'S NOTE: Eels are almost always sold skinned in the United States.

Floating island Gisou

Another old-fashioned recipe from Grandmother Bocuse. This floating-island dessert made with vanilla custard and slivered almonds is always a great success. I'm sure I don't have to tell you how good it is. Just the sight of it will make your mouth water.

The way the eggs are handled is at the heart of this recipe. The egg whites should never boil, but should be gently poached. The vanilla custard should not truly cook either, or you will have scrambled eggs flavored with vanilla.

You should take two other precautions in preparing this dessert: don't let the water in which you poach the egg whites boil or they will fall and soften; and be careful not to burn the caramel, which could give a bitter taste to this delicious dessert.

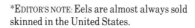

PEAS FRENCH-STYLE
Petits pois à la française

Ingredients for 4 people:

pounds fresh new peas
heads baby lettuce
–5 medium spring onions
ea salt
reshly ground pepper
tablespoons sugar
large pats of butter

Method:

1. Wash the peas, shell them, and emove the strings from the pods.
2. Wash and quarter the lettuce.

3. In a bowl, arrange the lettuce, the onions cut up into chunks, the peas, and the pods.

4. Season with salt and pepper, sprinkle with sugar, add the butter in little pieces.

5. Cover and allow to stand overnight in the refrigerator.
6. Transfer to a large saucepan, place a heatproof plate on top, and fill the plate with cold water or ice cubes. Simmer over moderate heat for 20 minutes.

7. Serve immediately in a shallow bowl.

EEL STEW
Matelote d'anguille

Ingredients for 4 people:

1 eel, about 2 pounds
sea salt
freshly ground pepper
8 tablespoons (1 stick) butter
¼ pound bacon
10 small onions
20 mushrooms
1 *bouquet garni*
1½ ounces cognac
1 bottle red wine
4 garlic cloves
4 eggs
¼ cup flour
several slices of country-style bread
1 garlic clove

Method:

1. Cut the skinned eel crosswise into 2-inch pieces; season with salt and pepper.
2. Melt 4 tablespoons of butter in a stew pot or casserole and sauté the eel until golden.
3. Add the bacon cut into small

pieces, the peeled onions, the mushrooms, and the *bouquet garni* and sauté.

4. Heat the cognac, pour into the pot, and flambé. Add the wine.

5. Add 4 garlic cloves, peeled and chopped, and simmer for 15 to 18 minutes.
6. Remove the eel and vegetables and keep warm.
7. Break the eggs one by one, slide each into the sauce, and poach for 3 to 4 minutes. Remove and keep warm.

8. Mix the rest of the butter and the flour to make a paste. Stir this into the sauce.
9. Arrange the eel, vegetables, and eggs on a serving platter. In a skillet fry the bread slices, rubbed with a cut clove of garlic, in a little butter. Serve the stew with the fried bread immediately.

FLOATING ISLAND GISOU
Oeufs à la neige Gisou

Ingredients for 4 people:

FOR THE VANILLA CUSTARD:

8 egg yolks
1 cup sugar
4 cups milk
1 vanilla bean

FOR THE "ISLANDS":

8 egg whites
1–2 tablespoons sugar
8 cups boiling salted water

TO SERVE:

slivered almonds
10–20 sugar cubes

Method:

1. In a bowl, mix together the egg yolks and sugar until foamy.
2. Split the vanilla bean, scrape the insides, and add the scrapings to the milk. Bring the milk to a boil in a saucepan.
3. Carefully add the milk to the egg yolk mixture.
4. Pour into a saucepan over very low heat and beat with a whisk until

the mixture thickens.
5. Pour into a cold bowl and allow to cool, beating constantly with a whisk.
6. For the "islands," beat the egg whites with the sugar until they

form stiff peaks.
7. In a saucepan, bring the lightly salted water to a boil. Lower the heat and poach the egg whites,

which have been formed into large balls, for 6 minutes, turning them after 3 minutes.

8. Drain the egg whites very carefully on a tea towel. Arrange on a serving platter, cover with the custard, and sprinkle with slivered almonds.
9. Caramelize the sugar cubes in a saucepan with a tablespoon of cold water. Pour the caramel over the "islands" and serve.

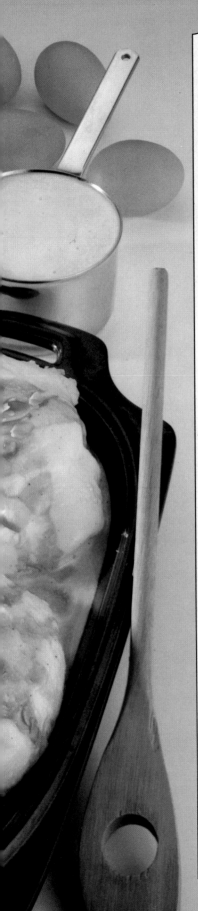

My advice

The wine regions of France

You need an entire lifetime to become familiar with all the various wines of France, to taste and appreciate them all.

Depending on the region and type of grape, the wines of France offer a whole palette of tastes that will satisfy the desires of everyone: light and fruity wines, robust and tannic wines, wines that age well and

wines to be drunk young. The richness of the French vineyards is that some wines share certain qualities, but no one wine is like another. Each person should develop his judgment and his preference for particular wines.

French wines are classified in three categories: table or country wines; VDQS, or Vins Délimités de Qualité Supérieure, wines of higher

quality; and AOC, or Appellations d'Origine Contrôlée, wines that come from a particular vineyard or chateau. Strict regulations determine the criteria for claiming one category or another.

The total wine production in France is 670 million liters, out of which only 170 million are AOC.

The map above shows the principal wine regions of France.

Asparagus vinaigrette

In my region of France, we use green-tipped asparagus from the south. One has a tendency to overlook the white-tipped asparagus, served mostly in the Alsace region with ham, a delicious dish.

The color of asparagus tips varies from pink to violet-blue to green, depending on the variety. That most commonly eaten in France is the green-tipped variety. Although we find asparagus from all over the world almost all year round, French asparagus is at its best from February until May.

You can recognize fresh asparagus by its cut end, which should be neither brittle nor dry, but firm and moist.

A vegetable peeler should be used to peel the asparagus stalk; hold the asparagus flat on your work surface while you peel it so that it won't break.

Pot-au-feu

This is a veritable national dish of France. It develops its best flavor when it is made in large quantities. The combination of meats, bones, poultry, and vegetables gives this specialty an incomparable flavor.

Choosing only the highest-quality ingredients will guarantee its success. The *pot-au-feu* is usually served in two different courses: first, the broth poured over toasted country-style bread, sprinkled with grated Swiss cheese; then, the meats surrounded by the vegetables as a main course.

Ask your butcher if he can give you 6 marrow bones. Before adding them to the *pot-au-feu,* seal the two ends of each bone with slices of potato and tie with kitchen string so the marrow remains intact.

Apple upside-down tart

There are as many recipes for this dessert as there are cooks. This one comes from my son-in-law, Jean-Jacques Bernachon. First you sauté the apples in the butter and sugar, then you cover them with the dough and place in the oven, and finally, you invert the tart onto a serving plate.

The *tarte Tatin* was "invented" not so very long ago by the Tatin sisters in their restaurant in Lamotte-Beuvron, in the Loir-et-Cher region. For this divine dessert, use Granny Smiths or other tart apples, but certainly not Golden Delicious.

While the apples cook, their juice caramelizes with the sugar and butter to color and envelop the fruit. This caramel should not be too thin or it will run when the tart is unmolded.

ASPARAGUS VINAIGRETTE
Asperges vinaigrette

Ingredients for 4 people:

2 pounds fresh asparagus
5 quarts cold water
3 tablespoons sea salt

FOR THE VINAIGRETTE:

1 egg white
1 tablespoon Dijon mustard
1 tablespoon wine vinegar
salt
freshly ground pepper
3–4 tablespoons olive oil
a few drops of Beaujolais

Method:

1. Carefully peel the asparagus stalks and tie into bundles with kitchen string.
2. Cut off the tough bottoms. Boil the asparagus in salted water for about 20 minutes.

3. To make the vinaigrette, combine the egg white, the mustard, and the vinegar.

4. Season with salt and pepper and add the olive oil at room temperature, drop by drop, beating constantly.
5. Add a few drops of Beaujolais to taste.

6. Remove the asparagus bundles from the water and rinse for a few

minutes under cool running water to retain their color. Drain on a tea towel.
7. Arrange the asparagus on a plate, cover with the sauce, and serve immediately.

POT-AU-FEU
Pot-au-feu

Ingredients for 4 people:

1 small beef knuckle
1 small veal knuckle
1 pound beef brisket
1 pound oxtail
1 stewing chicken (or hen)
5–6 quarts cold water
4 tablespoons sea salt
1 *bouquet garni*
1 leek
1 celery stalk
1 small cabbage
2 tomatoes
1 onion stuck with 3 cloves
6 marrow bones sealed with potato slices
1 whole kielbasa
1 small celery root
2 turnips
2 carrots
8 medium potatoes
1 bunch parsley
a few sprigs thyme
½ pound string beans

Method:

1. Place the meats in a large stew pot, fill with cold water, and bring to a boil, uncovered.

2. Carefully skim the top and lower the heat. Skim at intervals while the soup boils so that the broth will be clear.

3. Season with salt, add the *bouquet garni*, and simmer for 2 hours.

4. Meanwhile, peel and wash the leek, the celery stalk, the cabbage, and the tomatoes. Cut into chunks.

5. Stick the cloves in the onion, prepare the marrow bones, and set aside with the sausage.

6. Peel the celery root, the turnips, the carrots, and the potatoes and cut them into chunks.

7. After 2 hours, add all the vegetables (except the string beans), the sausage, and the thyme and parsley to the stew pot. Continue to simmer.

8. After a half hour, remove the chicken and veal knuckle and set aside in a bowl with a little broth, covered with a towel to keep warm.

9. Add the string beans, sliced into small pieces, 15 minutes later.

10. Serve the broth, then the meats surrounded by the vegetables. Serve with *cornichons* (little French pickles), coarse salt, and mustard.

APPLE UPSIDE-DOWN TART
Tarte Tatin

Ingredients for 4 people:

FOR THE PASTRY:

⅔ cup flour
pinch of sea salt
1 tablespoon sugar
6 tablespoons softened butter
1 egg yolk
1–2 tablespoons cold water

FOR THE FILLING:

3 pounds apples
14 tablespoons butter
⅓ cup sugar

Method:

1. To make the dough, pour the flour on your work surface and combine with the salt and sugar.
2. Add the butter and work the dough with your fingers.
3. Add the egg yolk and water and mix until you obtain a smooth dough. Allow to rest for an hour.

4. Peel, core, and quarter the apples.
5. Arrange the apple quarters closely to cover the bottom of a special copper Tatin pan, round-edged ovenproof pan, or skillet; add the butter, cut in pieces, between the apple quarters and pour the

sugar over the top.
6. Sauté slowly on top of the stove for 30 to 40 minutes.
7. Roll out the dough and cut it into a circle a little larger than the pan.

8. Remove the pan from the heat and cover the apples with the dough.

Press down the edges of the dough inside the rim of the pan to seal in the apples.
9. Bake in a preheated 400° oven for about 20 minutes, remove from the oven, invert onto a serving platter, and serve either hot or warm.

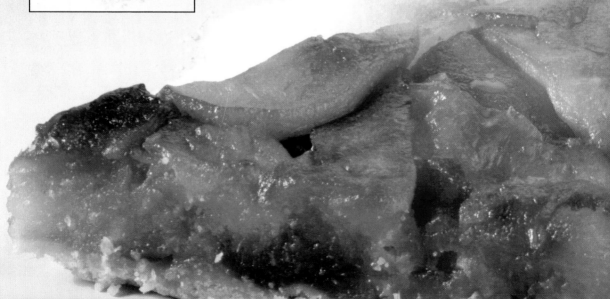

If you have good vintage wines at home, you should treat them with respect. The uncorking of the bottle is very important. First of all, cut the metal cover around the "ring" of the bottle's neck, so that the wine does not touch the lead or plastic

when it is poured. Now remove the cork with a corkscrew, being careful not to jar the bottle too much. Smell the cork: that is the only way to determine if the wine is still good.

Now it is time to decant the wine. Slowly pour it into a carafe. Hold the bottle in front of a candle or light. As any sediment reaches the neck of the bottle, stop pouring. It should be poured very slowly so that the oxygen can enrich it and so it can breathe fully. This should be done 2 hours before dining.

I am not a great supporter of decanting. My friend Monsieur Leroy of Romanée Conti never decants wine, even when it is very old. I once

drank an undecanted magnum of 1926 wine with him. What a delight!

More Cookbooks from Paul Bocuse

Paul Bocuse's French Cooking
(available in hardcover and paperback)

Paul Bocuse in Your Kitchen

ABOUT THE AUTHOR

In 1959, Paul Bocuse succeeded his father at the family restaurant in Collonges-au-Mont-d'Or, near Lyon. Within two years he had earned his first star and was named Meilleur Ouvrier de France cuisinier. His second and third stars quickly followed in 1962 and 1965.

Bocuse has circled the globe countless times teaching, lecturing, and practicing the fine art of cooking. He has established restaurants around the world. At his restaurant in Tokyo, he introduced his own contribution to French cooking, *nouvelle cuisine.* "Chefs de France," his restaurant at Epcot Center in Orlando, attracts almost three-quarters of a million people annually.

Internationally recognized as one of the greatest living chefs, Bocuse was made a member of the Légion d'honneur in recognition of his services as an ambassador of French cuisine. In 1986, he was named Gault-Millau Chef of the Year.